Master Your Money

A Simple 7-Step Budgeting System.

by
Steve Abraham

© 2024 Steve Abraham.
All rights reserved.

No part of this book may be reproduced, distributed, or transmitted in any form or by any means, including photocopying, recording, or other electronic or mechanical methods, without the prior written permission of the publisher, except in the case of brief quotations embodied in critical reviews and certain other noncommercial uses permitted by copyright law.

Dedication

To everyone striving to take control of their financial future, may this book be the guide that leads them to financial peace and prosperity?

Table of Contents

Introduction 1

STEP 1: Track Your Spending 2
    Why Tracking Your Spending Matters 2
    How to Track Your Spending 2
    Real-Life Example 3
    Tips for Effective Tracking 3

STEP 2 Categorize Your Expenses 4
    Importance of Categorization 4
    How to Categorize Your Expenses 4
    Real-Life Example 5
    Common Expense Categories 5
    Tips for Effective Categorization 6

STEP 3: Set Financial Goals 7
    The Role of Financial Goals 7
    Types of Financial Goals 7
    How to Set Financial Goals 8
    Real-Life Example 8
    Prioritizing Your Goals 8
    Tips for Achieving Your Goals 9

STEP 4: Create a Budget 10
    The Importance of a Budget 10
    How to Create a Budget 10
    Real-Life Example 11
    Budgeting Methods 11

   Tips for Effective Budgeting 11

STEP 5: Implement Your Budget 13
   The Challenge of Implementation 13
   How to Implement Your Budget 13
   Real-Life Example 14
   Tips for Successful Implementation 14
   Dealing with Challenges 14

STEP 6: Monitor and Adjust 16
   The Need for Monitoring 16
   How to Monitor Your Budget 16
   Real-Life Example 16
   Tips for Effective Monitoring 17
   Adjusting Your Budget 17

STEP 7: Review and Reflect 18
   The Importance of Reviewing 18
   How to Review Your Budget 18
   Real-Life Example 18
   Tips for Effective Reviewing 19
   Reflecting on Your Budget 19

Introduction

Managing your finances can seem daunting, but it doesn't have to be. With a straightforward and practical budgeting system, anyone can take control of their money and achieve financial peace.

This guide will walk you through a simple 7-step process to set up a budget that works for you, whether you're trying to pay off debt, save for a big purchase, or keep track of where your money goes. Let's dive in and start mastering your money today.

STEP 1
Track Your Spending

Why Tracking Your Spending Matters

The first step in creating a successful budget is understanding where your money goes. This foundational step is crucial because it clearly shows your financial habits and highlights areas where you might be overspending. Without this knowledge, making informed decisions about where to cut back or how to allocate your funds more effectively is challenging.

How to Track Your Spending

To track your spending effectively, commit to recording every expense for at least one month. Here's how you can do it:

1. **Collect Receipts**: Save all receipts from your purchases, no matter how small. This includes everything from your morning coffee to your utility bills.

2. **Use a Notebook or App**: Write down every purchase in a notebook or use a budgeting app to record your expenses. Apps like Mint, YNAB (You Need A Budget), or even a simple Excel spreadsheet can be beneficial.

3. **Categorize Expenses**: As you track your spending, immediately categorize each. Common categories include groceries, dining out, transportation, entertainment, and bills.

Real-Life Example

Sarah decided to track her spending for a month. She collected receipts from groceries, dining out, transportation, and entertainment. She also noted down her rent, utilities, and other recurring expenses. At the end of the month, she had a clear picture of her spending habits and realized she was spending more on dining out than she thought. This insight was crucial for adjusting her spending and creating a realistic budget.

Tips for Effective Tracking

1. **Be Consistent**: Make tracking your spending a daily habit. Set a reminder on your phone if needed.

2. **Involve the Whole Family**: If you share finances with a partner or family, ensure everyone is on board with tracking expenses. This will give you a more accurate picture of your household spending.

3. **Review Regularly**: Review your recorded expenses at the end of each week. This helps you understand your spending patterns and make the necessary adjustments.

By thoroughly tracking your spending, you lay the groundwork for the rest of your budgeting process. This step might seem tedious, but it's essential for creating a budget that truly reflects your financial situation.

STEP 2
Categorize Your Expenses

Importance of Categorization

Once you have tracked a month's worth of expenses, it's time to categorize them. Categorizing your expenses helps you see where most of your money is going and identifies areas where you can cut back. It's a critical step for gaining control over your finances.

How to Categorize Your Expenses

1. **List All Categories**: Start by listing all potential expense categories. Common categories include housing, utilities, groceries, dining out, transportation, entertainment, debt payments, insurance, and miscellaneous.

2. **Assign Each Expense**: Go through your tracked expenses and assign each one to the appropriate category. This may take some time, but seeing where your money is going is worth the effort.

3. **Total Each Category**: Once all expenses are categorized, total the amount spent in each category. This will give you a clear picture of your spending patterns.

Real-Life Example

Sarah took her tracked expenses and sorted them into categories. She discovered that her most significant expense was housing, groceries, and dining out. Entertainment and transportation were also substantial categories. This categorization helped her see the bigger picture and identify areas where she could potentially save money.

Common Expense Categories

1. **Housing**: Rent or mortgage, property taxes, home insurance.
2. **Utilities**: Electricity, water, gas, internet, phone.
3. **Groceries**: All food and household supplies purchased for home use.
4. **Dining Out**: Restaurants, cafes, fast food.
5. **Transportation**: Car payments, fuel, public transportation, maintenance.
6. **Entertainment**: Movies, concerts, subscriptions, hobbies.
7. **Debt Payments**: Credit card payments, loans, other debts.
8. **Savings and Investments**: Emergency fund, retirement accounts, other savings.
9. **Insurance**: Health, auto, life, and other insurance premiums.
10. **Miscellaneous**: Any other expenses that don't fit into the above categories.

Tips for Effective Categorization

1. **Be Honest**: Don't try to hide or ignore any expenses. Be honest with yourself about where your money is going.

2. **Use Subcategories**: If a category is too broad, break it down into subcategories. For example, "Entertainment" can be split into "Movies," "Games," "Concerts," etc.

3. **Adjust as Needed**: If you find that certain categories are too vague or too detailed, adjust them to better suit your needs.

Categorizing your expenses is a vital step in the budgeting process. It gives you a clear picture of your spending habits and highlights areas where you can make adjustments to achieve your financial goals.

STEP 3
Set Financial Goals

The Role of Financial Goals

Now that you know where your money is going, it's time to set some financial goals. Setting goals gives you a clear purpose and motivation for sticking to your budget. These goals can be short-term, like saving for a vacation, or long-term, like paying off debt or building an emergency fund.

Types of Financial Goals

1. **Short-Term Goals**: These are goals you want to achieve within the next year. Examples include saving for a vacation, buying a new gadget, or creating a small emergency fund.

2. **Medium-Term Goals**: These are goals you plan to achieve within the next 1-5 years. Examples include paying off significant debt, saving for a car, or building a more substantial emergency fund.

3. **Long-Term Goals**: These are goals that will take more than five years to achieve. Examples include saving for retirement, paying off a mortgage, or funding a child's education.

How to Set Financial Goals

1. **Be Specific**: Clearly define what you want to achieve. Instead of saying, "I want to save money," say, "I want to save $1,000 for an emergency fund."
2. **Make Them Measurable**: Ensure your goals have measurable outcomes. This helps you track your progress and stay motivated.
3. **Set a Time Frame**: Give yourself a deadline for achieving each goal. This creates a sense of urgency and helps you stay focused.
4. **Be Realistic**: Set goals that are challenging but achievable. Unrealistic goals can lead to frustration and discouragement.

Real-Life Example

Sarah set a goal to save $1,000 for an emergency fund within the next three months. She also aimed to pay off her credit card debt within a year. These goals gave her a clear direction and made her more committed to following her budget.

Prioritizing Your Goals

Not all goals can be achieved simultaneously, so it's essential to prioritize them. Decide which goals are most important and focus on those first. For example, building an emergency fund might take precedence over saving for a vacation.

Tips for Achieving Your Goals

1. **Break Goals into Smaller Steps**: Large goals can be overwhelming. Break them down into smaller, manageable steps. For example, if you want to save $1,000 in three months, aim to save about $333 monthly.

2. **Celebrate Milestones**: Recognize and celebrate when you reach milestones to achieve your goals. This will keep you motivated.

3. **Stay Flexible**: Life is unpredictable, and your goals may need to change over time. Be willing to adjust your goals as your financial situation evolves.

Setting financial goals is a crucial step in the budgeting process. Goals provide direction and motivation, helping you stay focused on what's most important. By setting specific, measurable, and realistic goals, you'll be well on your way to financial success.

STEP 4
Create a Budget

The Importance of a Budget

You can now create a budget with your expenses categorized and your financial goals set. A budget is a plan for how you will spend your money each month. It helps you ensure that your spending goes with your goals and that you're not spending more than what you earn.

How to Create a Budget

1. **List Your Income**: Start by listing all your income sources and total monthly income. This includes your salary, any side hustles, rental income, or any other source of regular income.

2. **Allocate to Categories**: Based on your tracked expenses and financial goals, allocate your income to each expense category. Make sure to prioritize essential expenses like housing, utilities, and groceries first.

3. **Prioritize Financial Goals**: After covering your essential expenses, allocate funds to your financial goals. These might include savings, debt repayment, or investments.

4. **Discretionary Spending**: Any remaining funds can be allocated to discretionary spending categories like dining out, entertainment, and hobbies.

Real-Life Example

Sarah created a budget by listing her monthly income from her job. First, she allocated funds for rent, utilities, groceries, and transportation. Then, she set aside money for her financial goals: saving for an emergency fund and paying off credit card debt. Finally, she allocated a small amount for dining out and entertainment, making sure her total expenses didn't exceed her income.

Budgeting Methods

1. **50/30/20 Rule**: This simple budgeting method suggests allocating 50% of your income to needs, 30% to wants, and 20% to savings and debt repayment.

2. **Zero-Based Budgeting**: In this method, you allocate every dollar of your income to an expense category until you have zero dollars left to budget. This ensures that you give every dollar a job.

3. **Envelope System**: This cash-based system involves putting cash for different spending categories into separate envelopes. Once the cash is gone, you can't spend any more in that category for the month.

Tips for Effective Budgeting

1. **Be Realistic**: Make sure your budget reflects your actual spending habits and income. An overly restrictive budget can be hard to stick to.

2. **Review Regularly**: Review your budget regularly and compare it to your actual spending. Adjust as necessary to stay on track.
3. **Automate Savings**: Set up automatic transfers to your savings account to ensure you're consistently saving towards your goals.

Creating a budget is a vital step in taking control of your finances. It helps you ensure that your spending aligns with your goals and that you're not living beyond your means. By following a structured approach to budgeting, you can create a plan that works for you and your financial situation.

STEP 5
Implement Your Budget

The Challenge of Implementation

Creating a budget is one thing; sticking to it is another. Implementing your budget requires discipline and regular monitoring. This step is about putting your budget into action and ensuring you follow the plan you've set.

How to Implement Your Budget

1. **Use Cash Envelopes**: For discretionary spending categories like dining out and entertainment, withdraw cash and place it in labeled envelopes. This helps you stick to your budget because once the cash is gone, you can't spend any more in that category.

2. **Leverage Technology**: Use budgeting apps or spreadsheets to track your real-time spending. Apps like Mint, YNAB, and EveryDollar can sync with your bank accounts and help you monitor your budget.

3. **Set Up Alerts**: Set up alerts for when you're close to reaching your budget limits in various categories. This can help prevent overspending.

Real-Life Example

Sarah decided to use the cash envelope method for her discretionary spending categories, such as dining out and entertainment. She withdrew cash at the beginning of the month and placed it in labeled envelopes. Once the cash was gone, she couldn't spend any more in that category. This helped her stick to her budget and avoid overspending.

Tips for Successful Implementation

1. **Stay Consistent**: Consistency is key to sticking to your budget. Make it a habit to record expenses daily and review your budget weekly.
2. **Involve Your Family**: If you share finances with a partner or family member, ensure everyone is on board with the budget. This will make it easier to stick to the plan.
3. **Be Flexible**: Life is unpredictable, and unexpected expenses will arise. Be flexible and adjust your budget as needed.

Dealing with Challenges

1. **Impulse Purchases**: To combat impulse purchases, implement a waiting period for non-essential items. If you still want the item after a week, consider buying it.
2. **Unexpected Expenses**: Build a buffer into your budget for unforeseen expenses. This can help you avoid dipping into savings or going into debt.
3. **Budget Fatigue**: Budgeting can feel restrictive. To avoid budget fatigue, allow yourself some fun money each

month. This small amount for guilt-free spending can keep you motivated.

Implementing your budget is where the real work begins. It requires discipline and commitment, but the rewards are worth it. By using tools like cash envelopes and budgeting apps, involving your family, and being flexible, you can successfully stick to your budget and achieve your financial goals.

STEP 6
Monitor and Adjust

The Need for Monitoring

Your budget is not set in stone. Life changes, and so should your budget. Monitoring and comparing your spending to your budget helps you stay on track and make necessary adjustments.

How to Monitor Your Budget

1. **Daily Check-Ins**: Spend a few minutes each day recording your expenses and reviewing your budget. This will keep you aware of your spending and help you catch any issues early.
2. **Weekly Reviews**: At the end of each week, review your spending in each category and compare it to your budget. This helps you see if you're on track or need adjustments.
3. **Monthly Assessments**: At the end of each month, compare your overall spending to your budget. Look for patterns and areas where you consistently overspend.

Real-Life Example

Halfway through the month, Sarah noticed she was spending more on groceries than she had budgeted. She adjusted her budget by reducing her dining out category and increasing her grocery category. This flexibility allowed her to stay on track with her overall budget.

Tips for Effective Monitoring

1. **Set Reminders**: Set reminders on your phone to review your budget regularly. This helps you stay consistent with your monitoring.
2. **Use Budgeting Tools**: Budgeting apps can provide real-time insights into your spending and help you monitor your budget more effectively.
3. **Stay Flexible**: Be willing to adjust your budget as needed. If you consistently overspend in one category, consider reallocating funds from another category.

Adjusting Your Budget

1. **Identify Problem Areas**: Look for categories where you consistently overspend. These are the areas that need adjustment.
2. **Reallocate Funds**: If you overspend in one category, try to cut back in another category to balance your budget.
3. **Update Your Goals**: As your financial situation changes, update your financial goals and adjust your budget accordingly.

Monitoring and adjusting your budget is a continuous process. It helps you stay on track and ensures your budget reflects your current financial situation. By regularly reviewing and adjusting your budget, you can control your finances and achieve your financial goals.

STEP 7
Review and Reflect

The Importance of Reviewing

At the end of each month, it's essential to review your budget and reflect on your progress. This step helps you understand what worked, what didn't, and how to improve your budgeting process.

How to Review Your Budget

1. **Compare Budget vs. Actuals**: Compare your actual spending to your budgeted amounts. Identify any discrepancies and understand why they occurred.
2. **Assess Goal Progress**: Review your progress towards your financial goals. Are you on track to achieve them? If not, what changes do you need to make?
3. **Identify Patterns**: Look for patterns in your spending. Are there areas where you consistently overspend or underspend?

Real-Life Example

At the end of the first month, Sarah reviewed her budget and saw that she had successfully saved $300 towards her emergency fund. She also noticed she didn't miss the extra dining out she had cut from her budget. This review motivated her to continue with her budget and set new goals for the upcoming month.

Tips for Effective Reviewing

1. **Be Honest**: Be honest with yourself about your spending habits and progress. This is crucial for making meaningful improvements.

2. **Celebrate Successes**: Celebrate your successes, no matter how small. Recognizing your achievements keeps you motivated.

3. **Learn from Mistakes**: If you didn't stick to your budget, understand why and learn from your mistakes. Adjust your budget or habits to avoid similar issues in the future.

Reflecting on Your Budget

1. **What Worked Well**: Identify what worked well in your budgeting process. What strategies helped you stay on track?

2. **What Needs Improvement**: Identify areas that need improvement. What challenges did you face, and how can you overcome them?

3. **Set New Goals**: Based on your review, set new financial goals for the next month. This keeps you focused and motivated.

Reviewing and reflecting on your budget is a crucial step in the budgeting process. It helps you understand your spending habits, celebrate successes, and learn from mistakes. By regularly reviewing your budget, you can continuously improve your financial situation and achieve your financial goals.

By following these seven steps, you'll be well on your way to mastering your money and achieving your financial goals. Remember, budgeting is a journey, not a destination. Be patient with yourself, stay committed, and celebrate your progress along the way.

www.ingramcontent.com/pod-product-compliance
Lightning Source LLC
Chambersburg PA
CBHW072058230526
45479CB00010B/1135